D0461349

Performing Arts

Acting: Stage & Screen

Art Festivals & Galleries:
The Art of Selling Art

Comedy & Comedians

Filmmaking & Documentaries

Music & Musicians

Painting

Performing Arts

Photography

Sculpting

Writing: Stories, Poetry, Song, & Rap

Performing Arts

Z.B. Hill

Mason Crest

Mason Crest
450 Parkway Drive, Suite D
Broomall, PA 19008
www.masoncrest.com

Printed and bound in the United States of America.

First printing
9 8 7 6 5 4 3 2 1

Series ISBN: 978-1-4222-3167-8
ISBN: 978-1-4222-3174-6
ebook ISBN: 978-1-4222-8711-8

Cataloging-in-Publication Data on file with the Library of Congress.

Contents

KEY ICONS TO LOOK FOR:

Text-Dependent Questions: These questions send the reader back to the text for more careful attention to the evidence presented there.

Words to Understand: These words with their easy-to-understand definitions will increase the reader's understanding of the text, while building vocabulary skills.

Series Glossary of Key Terms: This back-of-the book glossary contains terminology used throughout this series. Words found here increase the reader's ability to read and comprehend higher-level books and articles in this field.

Research Projects: Readers are pointed toward areas of further inquiry connected to each chapter. Suggestions are provided for projects that encourage deeper research and analysis.

Sidebars: This boxed material within the main text allows readers to build knowledge, gain insights, explore possibilities, and broaden their perspectives by weaving together additional information to provide realistic and holistic perspectives.

Words to Understand

props: Objects other than furniture or clothing used during a performance.

choreographing: Arranging the movements of a dance or other scene that requires complex motion.

script: The words of a film or play written out.

lyrics: The words of a song.

percussionists: Musicians who play drums or other instruments that involve striking an object.

digitized: Stored or created on a computer.

score: The music that goes along with another piece of art, such as a film or play.

Chapter One

Creating Performing Arts

When most people think of art, they usually think of painting or sculpture. Visual arts—art in the form of objects—often take center stage. But there's a whole other category of art called the performing arts. Music, dance, theater, acting, and more are considered performing arts. Performing artists use tools like instruments and their bodies to create art that can certainly be seen or heard but isn't a physical thing. For example, a dance is a piece of art, but you can't touch it.

Performing art also sometimes includes performance art. Although the two words are very similar, performance art is a specific type of performing art. In performance art, the artist uses her body and some **props** to make people think deeply.

While a conductor may not play an instrument during a concert, he plays an important role in the orchestra's performance.

Performing arts covers a very wide range of art. It can include classical music, opera, ballet, and musical theater, but it can also cover the art of celebrity musicians and actors. All these types of performance art entertain us, and they can also make us look at life in new ways and start to think differently. They convey different emotions and moods using instruments, voices, and gestures. That's the power of art!

THE PEOPLE WHO MAKE PERFORMING ARTS

There are many layers to performing arts, and lots of people who are involved. Most often, people think of the actors, dancers, musicians, and singers who do the actual performing. They are definitely an important part of performing art, because without their talents, there wouldn't be any performing arts!

But these arts also depend on another set of people too. Someone has to create the design for the art in the first place by *choreographing* the dance, composing the music, or writing the *script*. Then someone has to direct the whole thing, moving the dancers, conducting the musicians, and advising the actors. Usually, all these people are considered artists to a certain extent. The director of your favorite movie is an artist just like the actors in it, but he contributes something different to the final product.

Make Connections: More People

All the people involved in performing art aren't considered artists, but that doesn't make them any less important. Lighting crews, camera operators, box office attendants, and ushers are all key to a smooth presentation of performance art.

Performing art often takes place on a stage, with an audience.

Each production of performing art may include one, two, or many performing artists. A movie usually has at least three or four main actors, while a theater production might have just one. A concert may feature one singer playing guitar or a whole orchestra made up of a hundred musicians.

WHERE IT HAPPENS

Most performing art happens in front of an audience, although there are plenty of exceptions. Plays, musical performances, and dance routines are done for live audiences. The audience often sits in a theater, watching the performance happen on stage.

Of course, actors can also act on a movie or TV screen. Some TV sets have live audiences, but most of the time actors are creating their art for an audience that will watch after the movie or show is edited into a final format.

Performing artists also spend many hours practicing their art in music practice rooms, in dance studios, at home, or backstage. And the people who create the art itself may also work in many different places. Only the final production of performing art happens on stage!

TYPES OF PERFORMING ART

Performing art covers a wide range of types of performances. Acting of all kinds involves portraying a person other than yourself. The actor must take on the mannerisms, behaviors, language, and emotions of the person she's acting out. Each actor's interpretation of the same role will be a little different. Shakespeare's play *Hamlet*, for example, has had thousands of productions since it was written, but each actor who plays the title character plays him a little bit differently. One actor might portray Hamlet as more sad, while another plays him as more angry. The unique portrayals are part of the actor's art.

Actors work in a variety of performing arts fields. They act in Broadway

Ballet is one kind of performing art that has been around for a long time.

Actors are performing artists, but their art may be viewed on screen, while their audiences sit in a movie theater—or their home living rooms.

and off-Broadway productions of plays. They act in the movies. They act on TV shows. Actors who are also talented singers act in musical theater shows, singing some of their scenes instead of speaking them.

Music is another broad category of performing arts. You might think mostly of symphony orchestras or operas when you think of art and

Research Project

This chapter outlines some of the differences between performing arts and visual arts. Do some more research on the line between these art forms by looking online or using the library. When did people first start using the term "performing arts"? Has the meaning changed over time? Can you find any examples of art that blurs the lines between performing and visual arts?

music. These kinds of music certainly are art, but there are others as well. For example, rap and pop music could also be considered under the performing arts umbrella. Some music has **lyrics** while other music does not. In either case, music is meant to make people feel emotions like excitement or sadness. Some music tells stories, or it speaks out for the rights of a group of people.

Singers, pianists, violinists, clarinetists, and **percussionists** all use different instruments to make their musical art. Some musical artists just rely on computers to make **digitized** music, without ever picking up an instrument.

Dance is a third major form of performing art that involves moving the body to express emotions or stories. Major dance forms include ballet, jazz, hip-hop, tap, and interpretive, among others. Dancers usually move to some music, so multiple kinds of performing art is combined into one. Ballets have dancers on stage, but they also often have a full orchestra playing the musical **score** to the ballet below the stage.

Text-Dependent Questions

1. What are four main types of performing arts?
2. What makes performing arts different from visual arts like painting or sculpting?
3. Where do the performing arts usually take place?
4. What sorts of musicians do we consider artists?
5. How is performance art different from the other performing arts?

Performance art is another type of non-visual art. It is rarely performed on stage in front of an audience. Instead, it might happen in a museum or even on the street. Performance art focuses on the artist's actions. The actions are the art because they force people to think about things differently. A lot of performance art is shocking or uncomfortable, and performance artists are sometimes willing to put themselves at great risk for their art.

Words to Understand

improvised: Made up on the spur of the moment.

universal: Able to be understood by everyone, regardless of when they live or where they are from.

melodramas: Stories with exaggerated emotions.

technologies: New inventions that humans create to make things easier or to do new things.

sinews: Tough fibers from inside an animal's body.

Chapter Two

The History
of Performing Arts

The history of performing arts is really the history of theater, music, dance, and more. Sometimes those separate histories come together for a time, as in the case of musical theater or ballet. Tracing the history of the performing arts isn't quite like doing the same for visual arts. Archaeologists and historians can use actual art like cave paintings and sculptures to trace the history of culture's visual arts. Performing arts don't leave any physical trace, though. Instead, researchers have to rely on accounts of performing arts in books and other texts. Historians may learn about performing arts from ancient drawings of them. Although we haven't learned everything there is to know about the history of performing arts, we can fill in a big part of their story.

This a reconstruction of the Globe Theatre's stage, where Shakespeare's plays were first acted.

THEATER

Theater is the art of acting out stories for an audience. Prehistoric people most likely acted out stories for each other, but it wasn't formal theater.

The Greeks are credited with creating the first theater. In fact, theater comes from a Greek word theasthai, which means "to behold." The Greeks came up with the idea of dividing theater into two types—comedy and tragedy. Comedic plays are funny, while tragic plays involve suffering and death.

The Romans adopted lots of Greek ideas, including theater. They

Make Connections

Shakespeare used language creatively when he wrote his plays. He created a lot of common English expressions still used today, such as "all of a sudden" and "fair play."

translated Greek theater into Latin and created their own plays. The Romans built huge theater buildings for the large audiences that attended plays.

There is also evidence that people were performing theater in early India. Sanskrit theater started about 100 CE and lasted all the way until the 1500s. This type of theater is called Sanskrit because that is the name of the language it was performed in. It was made up of religious plays that tell of kings' and gods' adventures.

In Europe during the Middle Ages, people didn't perform theater in actual buildings. Instead, traveling actors walked from city to city, putting on plays. Churches also put on plays that were meant to teach Christians biblical stories. There were professional actors now, people who dedicated their lives to acting and made money from it. A little later on, European theater also included "commedia dell'arte." For this Italian style of theater, there was a set cast of characters. The actors **improvised**, though, so the plays were never the same twice.

In the 1500s, one of the most famous playwrights to ever live came along. William Shakespeare was born in 1564 in England. He started off as an actor and a poet. Not much is known about his early life, except that he got married, had children, and eventually moved to London. By the late 1500s he belonged to a group of actors called the King's Men. He started publishing his poems and his plays, and became more

Alfred Hitchcock is remembered for the scary, suspenseful movies he created.

well known. In 1599, he helped build a theater in London called the Globe Theater.

People still read Shakespeare's plays today because they contain **universal** themes of love, tragedy, anger, and more. People related to his plays in the sixteenth century, and they still can relate to them today (as long as they can figure out the old language). People around the world have watched or read Shakespeare's plays translated into dozens of languages.

In Japan in the 1600s, a popular kind of theater was called "kabuki." A woman named Izumo no Okuni created kabuki, and it was soon a hit. Each play is based on a legend and contains instrumental music and dancing along with the acting. The actors wear elaborate makeup and costumes, which adds to the sense of shock and oddness that kabuki creates. Kabuki is still performed in Japan and other countries today.

Theater in the recent past has ranged from plays that tell historic stories to **melodramas** about love. Writers and actors from all over the world bring theater to life. Musical theater has become popular. Today, some of the newest and best plays can be seen on Broadway in New York City. You don't need to go to New York, though, to see good theater. Smaller professional theaters and even high school auditoriums put on plays for everyone to see.

FILM AND TV

Although theater acting has been around for a long time, film and TV acting are pretty new. The first moving pictures weren't invented until the 1890s. A French man named Louis Lumiere is usually given the credit for inventing the first camera to take moving pictures, but he relied on lots of knowledge and other inventions that came before him. Other people were also inventing similar **technologies** at the same time as Lumiere. His invention was called the Cinematograph.

The first "movies" were really just theater acts captured on the newly invented moving picture cameras. After a few years, filmmakers started playing around with camera techniques. The first real films shown in movie theaters were silent and in black and white. Filmmakers and scientists hadn't figured out how to add sound or color elements yet. Sometimes a live orchestra would play in the theater to accompany the movie.

Sound was added to movies in 1927. Color film had been invented before, but it only became cheap enough and easy enough to use in the 1930s.

Meanwhile, television was also taking off. Lots of people had been working on the idea of television for several decades by the time the first TV picture was produced in 1927. In the 1940s, televised news, sports games, and other entertainment started taking the place of the radio. Early TV programs came on air, and everyone wanted a TV. After World War II, more and more households had at least one TV. Every decade saw new TV shows and better picture quality, all the way up to today.

Soon after film and TV was invented, screen actors started becoming celebrities. The stars were considered artists, and their non-screen lives became the subject of entertainment. Movie and TV stars are of the most recognizable people today. Some of the people behind the scenes also became famous. Directors and producers like Steven Spielberg, George Lucas, and Alfred Hitchcock are all well known for the movies they created.

DANCE

Dancing probably was created long, long ago as part of spiritual ceremonies. Prehistoric people would dance to communicate with spirits or gods. Dancing is still used this way today by some people.

Early recorded forms of dancing include Egyptian priests and priestesses dancing for gods during rituals. Egyptian women also danced during funerals. Scientists have found paintings of dancers in Egyptian tombs, showing that dance was an important part of life. Meanwhile, early Greeks danced in front of newly completed temples, while in India, priestesses danced by Hindu temples. The Greek philosopher Aristotle

Make Connections

There are hundreds of different kinds of dancing in the world, from lots of different countries. Here are just a few:

- Contra: A kind of folk dance from New England in which people are partnered up and travel down a line of other pairs. A caller at the front of the dance hall yells out which moves to do. Musicians play music on fiddles, guitars, and other folk instruments. Contra dancing comes from European line dancing traditions.
- Swing: A partner dance done to jazz music and rooted in African American dances. Swing dancing was most popular in the early twentieth century, although people still go to swing dances today.
- Bhangra: Dancing from the Punjab region of India. Bhangra has gone through many forms, from a folk dance used to celebrate the harvest to a more modern style that has mixed with other styles of dancing and recorded music. Indian immigrants and their children around the world practice Bhangra.
- Flamenco: Flamenco comes from southern Spain and includes a specific style of singing, guitar playing, and clapping. One or two people dance at a time; women usually wear long, ruffled dresses. Flamenco has roots in gypsy (Roma) culture and from the Moors, Islamic residents of the area.
- Salsa: A partner dance first created in New York City, but heavily influenced by Latin American forms of dancing. Dancers usually dance to salsa music; the dance involves fancy footwork.

compared dancing to poetry because of its ability to communicate emotions and ideas.

One of the dance forms most often associated with art is ballet. Ballet was first developed in Italy during the Renaissance, and then traveled to France. The first professional ballet dancers belonged to the Paris Opera

When the Beatles arrived in America in 1964, they brought with them a brand-new sound and look. People didn't know what to think about this new art form.

Ballet, which was set up by King Louis the XVI. Ballet eventually became popular in Russia, the United States, Australia, and other countries. Composers created musical works to go along with big ballet productions, combining orchestras and dancing. Many of those ballets are still performed today. One of the most famous is Tchaikovsky's *The Nutcracker*. Some ballet dancers today build on traditional dance techniques, but they have created a new kind of dance called contemporary ballet that involves different movements.

One of the most recently invented dance forms is hip-hop. In the

1970s, a few African American musical artists started creating a new kind of music and culture called hip-hop. Unlike some other forms of dance, hip-hop was created on the street rather than in a studio or a professional dance company. One of the biggest influences on early hip-hop dance and music was DJ Kool Herc, a DJ from the Bronx in New York City.

Kool Herc (whose real name was Clive Campbell) was born in Jamaica but came to the United States in 1967. He threw block and house parties in the Bronx, using mostly funk music. His real innovation was focusing on the break in each song—the part where the vocals drop out, leaving only drums or other instruments. People started dancing to the break in a style known as breakdancing. The dancers, who were called b-boys and b-girls, performed a lot of fancy footwork, dancing on the ground, and stunts like backflips. Hip-hop dancing is usually improvised, but it can also be choreographed for dance shows and concerts. Rap is also part of the hip-hop music tradition.

MUSIC

Music is one of the art forms with the longest history. We don't know just how long people have been singing and playing music, but it has certainly been a long time. People have come up with some theories. One theory supposes that babies learned to imitate their mothers' voices and the way they talk. Think of how adults often make their voices high and musical when they see a baby or a small animal. Other theories guess that people learned music from the rhythms of nature, like waves or even bird song. Maybe early people tried to imitate the sounds they heard every day all around them.

The first musical instruments were probably drums. Archaeologists have found very old drums—even one from 6000 BCE! These early drums were simple at first, just hollowed out tree trunks with animal skin stretched over them. Next, people started creating wind instruments, which are fairly easy to make by putting holes in a long, hollow tube

Living statues like this woman are a form of performance art. They are designed to make people react in some way.

like a reed. Flutes made of wood and bone that are thousands of years old have been found in China. Stringed instruments took a little more creativity. The first stringed instruments were made of animal *sinews* stretched on to a bow-shaped piece of wood. Early musicians probably just plucked the strings and later moved on to creating bows that could be moved across the strings to make a different sound.

As human history moved on, different groups of people created varying styles of music and lots of different instruments. We can't know exactly what early music sounded like, before it was written down or

Make Connections

Music isn't just beautiful—it's also based on math. The Greek thinker Pythagoras was the first recorded person to figure out the mathematical formulas behind music. He used strings to study musical notes, and eventually understood that the notes each string produced depended on how much it vibrated. The strings vibrate with different frequencies. Some of the frequencies are pleasant to hear and some are not. The frequency of vibration is determined by how long the string is, how tightly it is stretched, and what it is made of. Pythagoras came up with some mathematical formulas to describe those relationships.

recorded. Ancient music probably varied widely, from China to Europe to the Americas.

The first evidence for written music is from ancient Sumer (present-day Iraq). The Greeks, Byzantines, and Arabs also had their own styles of writing music. The current musical system used today was invented about a thousand years ago in Europe.

The history of music contains thousands and thousands of artists. Even such different musical artists as Beethoven and the Beatles are still all considered artists. Beethoven was a composer who was born in Germany in 1770 and lived in Vienna, Austria. He created classical works of music for orchestras, quartets, soloists, and more. The Beatles on the other hand, were musical performers as well as music writers who were popular in the 1960s. They wrote and performed rock-and-roll hits for audiences around the world. Although both Beethoven and the Beatles produced very different music in different eras, they both created art that is still appreciated today.

Research Project

Choose one performing artist of your choice. Pick your favorite musician, actor, dancer, or other performing artist. Do research on this person's life and how he or she fits into the performing arts in general. First, write a paragraph or two about the artist's life and work. Then write a paragraph about how the artist relates to his or her type of performing art, and how he or she influenced other artists of the same type.

PERFORMANCE ART

Performance art has a somewhat shorter history than other kinds of non-visual arts. The first people to experiment with performance arts were artists in the early 1900s. During that time period, painters and sculptors were playing with the ideas of art. For a long time, artists in Europe and North America mainly followed the same rules. But after World War I, people felt like they looked at the world differently because something so horrible had happened. They wanted to use art to explore new ideas and new ways of understanding the world.

So some artists started to expand what art could be. They thought it could include performance. In 1952, a composer called John Cage held a special experimental art event at Black Mountain College. Artists did performance art right in the middle of the audience! Other artists were inspired by this event, and more and more performance art was created. One example is called Composition for Pianoforte, performed by Nam June Paik. Paik played some music, then jumped off the stage and cut someone's tie off. Then he ran out of the building.

Text-Dependent Questions

1. Into what categories did the Greeks divide their plays?
2. Why are Shakespeare's plays still read and considered important today, a hundreds of years after he wrote them?
3. How did prehistoric and ancient people use dance?
4. What is one theory about how music was invented?
5. Why did artists develop performance art in the twentieth century?

In the 1970s, performance artists began using the body more as part of their art. In *Five-Day Locker Piece*, artist Chris Burden spent five days in a gym locker, only consuming water. And that was only one of the less extreme pieces! Performance art may seem silly, dangerous, or extreme, but it definitely makes people think. It often makes people react strongly in ways that paintings or sculpture don't.

Make Connections: Marina Abramovic

Perhaps the most famous performance artist is Marina Abramovic. She was born in Serbia and later moved to Amsterdam and to the United States. Abramovic's pieces have involved hurting herself and testing the limits of the human body. She almost died during one performance which involved leaping across flames into a container. In 2010, the Museum of Modern Art in New York City put on a show of Abramovic's previous works. As part of the show, she sat at a table in silence and invited museum visitors to sit across from her.

Words to Understand

dedicated: Devoted to something; willing to do anything to make it work.

agents: People who get work for artists such as actors and musicians.

network: Meet and become friends with other people in your industry who might be able to help your career.

supplement: Complete something or make something better.

Chapter Three

The Business of Performing Arts

The performing arts can be a business as well as an art. Hobby dancers or musicians can afford not to treat their art as a business, because they don't spend a lot of time doing it. They have other things to do like another job or school. But people who are very *dedicated* to their art and want to spend their lives doing it have to think in a more businesslike manner in order to make a living. Whether an artist is a professional movie director or a singer, being a businessperson is every bit as important as being an artist.

If you're serious about your art, you'll practice every chance you get. The only way you'll be able to build a career in performing arts is by getting better and better at your art—and the only way to get better is by practicing!

THE WORK BEHIND THE PERFORMANCE

Being a performing artist isn't actually all about giving performances. Artists also need to practice a lot. They also have to pay attention to the business aspects of their art. They need to find jobs and get hired to perform. They need to market themselves so that the general public knows who they are. While it's fun to imagine that performing artists lounge around all day, give a performance every so often while they make a lot of money, that's just not true.

Movie and film actors must constantly look for new work. If they're successful or can afford it, they can hire **agents** to help them. Otherwise, they have to scour ads and **network** with other theater, film, or television professionals to find opportunities for work. Then they need to audition, over and over again, to get those jobs. And if an actor gets an acting job, then he needs to practice and research, a lot. In order to play his character well, he might need to do some research. For example, if the actor is playing a businessman from the 1950s, he should research the time period and how people in business acted and what they did. He'll also need to memorize his lines and the movements he's supposed to do on stage or in front of the camera. All that is a lot of work!

Dancers follow a similar path. They must look for new dance productions to perform in, depending on what kind of dance they do. Dancers may end up working for theaters, for dance troupes, as backup dancers for musical artists, and even in places like cruise ships or casinos. They might also hop around from temporary dance job to dance job, if they like variety or if they can't find a more permanent position.

Musicians have many different options for job paths. Classically trained musicians who are particularly talented can look for a position with a symphony orchestra, a band, an opera company, or a choir. They might also play with smaller ensembles, like quartets, and look for soloist jobs playing with orchestras. Other musicians may form a band, or a solo act and look for gigs at concert venues, cafes, and clubs. They may travel from place to place on tour, no matter what kind of musician they

Auditioning for a role in a play can be scary. The more often you do it, though, the easier you'll find it.

are. And when they're not performing or looking for work, musicians are practicing!

Most musicians (and other performing artists) will need to work nights at some point, since that's when shows usually are performed. For all

Make Connections

Every year, the performing arts management industry holds a conference. Conferences are meant as a space for people in an industry to come together from across the country and sometimes the world to share ideas and learn new things. In 2014, the Performing Arts Manager Conference offered opportunities to learn about new student research in the field, outdoor event planning, expanding food services, weather and disaster preparedness, and sponsorship. Conference attendees could also visit the local ballet, museums, and theaters.

types of performing artists, work schedules can vary quite a lot. Even if an artist has a permanent job, her schedule will change based on performances. One week might be very, very busy, with rehearsals leading up to a major performance or tour. The week or month of the performance might require her to work Friday and Saturday nights. Then after the performance is over, the workload might be lighter for a little while. And artists who go from job to job never know what their schedules will look like. It all depends on when auditions are, and if they get work. An artist might not have any work for a month as he searches for auditions, but then work almost every day for three months after a successful audition. Performing artists have to be willing to be flexible with their schedules.

PERFORMING ARTS MANAGEMENT

Being the performer isn't the only option when it comes to performing arts. The arts administration business involves a lot of people who love art but who don't necessarily create it themselves.

Performing arts administrators work behind the scenes in theaters, concert venues, non-profits, and universities. Think of a theater that hosts a symphony orchestra. Hundreds of people may work at that theater.

Many performing artists teach classes to make ends meet while working in the arts.

Some sell tickets, or run the box office. Others design and maintain the theater's website. A marketing department runs the advertisements and creates the programs. Still others run auditions, make sure the music is ordered, and coordinate visiting musicians' schedules. There's a lot to do at a theater besides perform! The people in charge of all of those things fall into the category of performing arts management.

TEACHING

Many people who start out in performing arts realize that they want to become teachers. Succeeding in performing arts is hard, and becoming a teacher is a great alternative because there are more job openings. Plus, many artists realize they want to spread their art to new generations, and they truly love teaching.

Teachers can teach any form of performing art, and they can choose from a wide variety of teaching positions. Some teachers may want to help students who are just starting out, so they teach community classes or at elementary schools. Other teachers want to focus on students who are developing their skills, so they become middle or high school teachers. Still others want to work with students who are close to becoming professionals and teach at the college level or beyond.

Even artists who regularly perform may also be teachers. Most classically trained musicians, for example, have at least a student or two on the side. Teaching students lets artists earn some extra money, while filling up time that isn't spent in rehearsal, practicing, or giving performances.

SETTING UP A PERFORMING ARTS BUSINESS

Performing artists can work for someone or something else, like a theater, but they can also work for themselves. Out of all the performing arts, musicians are the ones most likely to actually set up their own business. A musician with a band should treat it as a business, even if the band is only him.

Some performers work in smaller, more intimate venues. Sometimes, it may be easier to get gigs in smaller places.

Treating performing art like a business helps an artist to find work, get more people to recognize her, and manage her money. The business side of performing arts can be a lot of work, but it can also be fun and rewarding. The better business skills an artist has, the more likely it is she'll be successful.

The business of performing art involves more than just the art. Artists must advertise their services and their names. They must actively search for new work. An artist who plays the cello, for example, might start his own music business. If he's not quite good enough to play in a major symphony orchestra, he still may have plenty of talent to play music in other places. He could find work playing at weddings and other gigs. He could offer lessons to beginning and advanced students. He could play in occasional orchestras that need some extra help. But he has to do some extra work to get all these jobs, or no one will know he exists.

HOW MUCH?

Some beginning performing artists dream of being as rich and famous as the artistic celebrities in the news and on stage or the screen. However,

Make Connections

All performing artists should also have a website to actively market themselves. Websites and social media help artists get their names out so they can get jobs. Websites should include background information on the artists' lives, education, and job experience, along with examples of their work. Artists could post videos of their performances, or mp3s if they are musicians. Contact information is also important. Then, if people are looking for information about that particular artist, they can visit the website to learn more about her and also find a way to get in contact with her if needed.

Even if you can't get a job in the performance yet, working in the box office is a way to earn money while being around the art you love. You may be able to find out about other opportunities as well.

While not every artist will become rich and famous from their art, performing and creating art can be its own reward.

most performing artists won't reach this kind of success, and many won't be able to make much money at all. But with hard work and determination—and some skill and luck—performing artists can make a decent living through their work.

The U.S. Bureau of Labor Statistics breaks down expected earnings of performing artists by category. The Bureau lists the average pay and what the bottom and top 10 percent earned in 2012. Most artists earn

Research Project

Do some research on the incomes of people in performing arts who are not performers. Check online or even in job advertisements to see how much performance arts managers, composers, play writers, theater directors, teachers, and others make per year. Write down what you find, and compare the numbers. Which jobs pay the most? Which pay the least? Do you think income is the only thing that matters when choosing a job? What else might people involved in the performing arts consider?

somewhere around the average, though they might also earn a lot less or a lot more. Here are the numbers:

Actors:
Average: $20.26 an hour
Bottom 10 percent: less than $8.92 an hour
Top 10 percent: more than $90.00 an hour

Dancers:
Average: $14.16 an hour
Bottom 10 percent: less than $8.50 an hour
Top 10 percent: more than $33.34 an hour

Musicians and singers:
Average: $23.50 an hour
Bottom 10 percent: less than $8.81 an hour
Top 10 percent: more than $65.24 an hour

Text-Dependent Questions

1. How do actors find new work?
2. What sort of schedule might a musician with a band have?
3. What do performing art managers do? Where do they work?
4. Why should performing artists consider their work as a business?
5. What was the average pay for a dancer in 2012? What about the pay for the bottom and top 10 percent of dancers?

Some artists, especially those who are just starting out, have a second job to **supplement** their art job. They may have jobs that have nothing to do with performing arts, like being a waiter or a clerk at a grocery store. Or they may find a job that is related to their art. They might work at a theater box office, a dance shop, or a record store. The experience they get at those sorts of jobs can help them figure out how to navigate the performing arts world.

Chapter Four

How Do I Get Involved in the Performing Arts?

The performing arts is one of the hardest professions to get into. Only the best of the best end up actually performing or creating performing art. Many people are weeded out along the way. It can be frustrating looking for work and auditioning, while trying to improve your artistic skills. Some people who start out trying to become performing artists end up moving into a slightly different field, like performing arts management or teaching. They realize that while they love their art, they also may never become a successful performing artist and that they also enjoy doing other things.

Don't be discouraged if you're just starting out in the performing arts. Just keep in mind that very few people actually become performing

Community and high school plays are a great way to get some experience on the stage.

Taking music classes in school and playing with others can help prepare you for a job as a musician later in life.

artists, and even fewer become famous. If you keep reality in mind, and work hard to improve your skills and get to know the right people, you can find the right career path for you.

EDUCATION

Most performing artists have some sort of educational background in their art. If you can, start taking classes in your chosen art now. You can look for classes in several places. Your school might offer some classes, particularly music and theater. Take orchestra, band, or chorus, for example. High schools often offer even more specialized classes in the performing arts. You'll get the direction and advice of a teacher

There are lots of behind-the-scenes jobs on a movie set.

showing you how to play an instrument, sing, or act. If you're interested in performance art, take a visual art class so you get to know the art world.

You should also look into community classes. If your school doesn't offer the particular kind of performing art you're interested in, see if an organization in your community offers it instead. If there's a theater or a music school around, sometimes they have programs for people in the community. If you can't afford the classes, check with the program to see if it offers scholarships or discounts. Any way you can learn your performing art early on is a good opportunity.

Private lessons are also a good idea. Musicians often take lessons from a young age so that they get better and better. One-on-one teaching is probably the best way to learn an instrument or improve your singing. You might also be able to find dance or acting lessons. Individual lessons are not as common in these areas, though.

You should also look into summer educational programs. Music, dance, and acting camps are popular around the country. Summer programs run for a week or more and offer intensive training in performing arts along with some fun. Camps are great because you're surrounded by other people who care passionately about the same things you do.

To become a professional performing artist, you may need to go to an art school for college. Musicians go to music school, even the artists who want to perform popular music forms rather than classical music or opera. To become an actor, you can choose to get a degree in theater or drama. However, many movie and TV stars didn't go to college for acting; instead, they started looking for work right after high school, or got a different degree in college. Dancers also don't necessarily go to college to get a dance degree, although some schools offer it.

Movie directors, conductors, composers, and other behind-the-scenes artists involved in the performing arts also often choose to get a college degree in their field. College courses can teach students about movie production, filming, writing music, and more.

Regular practice is a huge part of making a career in the performing arts, whether music, dance, or acting.

A degree in performing arts management may include courses in marketing, business and accounting, and statistics. Managers need a wide range of skills to successfully direct performing arts programs. A performing arts management degree opens the door to lots of careers. You might consider theater administration, music publishing, concert promotion, or representing an artist as an agent.

PRACTICE

Be prepared to practice when you take performing arts classes. It's not enough to just go to class once or twice a week. To get better and someday become a professional artist, you'll need to practice a lot.

Set up a routine, to make practicing a little easier. You might decide to practice three times a week for an hour after dinner, or twice a week for half an hour when you get home from school and two hours every weekend. You should set up a space for practicing that feels comfortable. You don't want to practice in your living room if your sibling is going to yell at you all the time to stop. The more you practice, the better you'll get. It will all really pay off when you're older and becoming a professional.

Take every opportunity you can find to practice and perform. Try out for your school play. Join a community or youth orchestra. Sing in front of an audience at a local café that puts on shows. Any way you can practice performing, especially in front of an audience, will help prepare you for the future.

LOOKING FOR WORK

If you're looking for work in the performing arts, don't expect it to be too easy. Finding a job can be tough and you'll have to be patient. Looking for performing arts work involves a lot of auditions. Musicians must audition to get into orchestras or to play at a particular venue. Dancers must audition to join a dance troupe or particular production.

Networking means you reach out to other people wherever and whenever you can. You never know when a friend of a friend of a friend might end up being the person who gives you your first big job as a performing artist!

As a young person, you have some options to get experience in the performing arts. While you're probably not looking for a full-time job, you can still find some jobs (even some paying ones!) that will introduce you to the hunt for work. If you play in an orchestra or dance with a troupe, people might sometimes come to your group and tell your director that they need some artists for an event. Maybe they need a quartet to play at a party, or a small group of dancers to perform at an art gallery opening. Sign up!

The more people who know you're an artist, the more likely it is that you'll get some work. If people come to you with jobs, you'll need to spend less energy on looking for work, and you'll have more time for getting better at your art. You could post flyers around town, or advertise in the newspaper or online. Someone might see your add and hire you for their own event.

Performing artists who create the art, like writers or choreographers, must also go through a long process to get work. For most performing artists behind the scenes, starting out is hard. If you are writing music or a play, you probably won't be able to get professional performers to do it, at least not yet. Try your work on your friends first. Put on your own play in your house or in a park. Choreograph a dance for the school talent show. Have your band play your new composition.

SETTING UP A BUSINESS

Young performing artists who want to set up their own art businesses should follow a few steps. First, decide how much time you can spend on your business. If you're a student, you can't dedicate yourself to a full time job yet. But you can put aside some time in the evenings, on the weekends, and in the summers.

Next, think about creating a business plan. These plans lay out what you want your business to look like, and what you want to do with it. You could just start a business without any planning, but you'll most likely

Jot down all your ideas for a business. Don't worry about putting them in order at first; just let your imagination flow. Draw pictures if that helps! Then when you're done, you can put it all together into an organized plan.

be more successful if you plan. At the very least, you'll need to tell other people about what your business is, and a business plan helps you think through all of that before you start explaining it to someone else.

You'll also need to decide if you're working alone or with someone

Make Connections: The Elements of a Business Plan

 Business plans are important when starting a business. They force you to consider all the different parts of your business and plan ahead, instead of just jumping in. Businesses tend to be much more successful when their owners take the time to plan. Your business plan doesn't have to be set in stone; you can change it as time goes on and your business begins to look different. But to start off, you should include:

- Summary. If someone doesn't have enough time to read the whole plan, he can just read the summary to get a quick overview.
- Objectives/goals. What do you hope to do with your business? How will you know when you're successful?
- Your mission. This is the reason your business exists, and why you started it in the first place. Your mission should be more than just making money.
- The target audience. Who are you trying to sell your art to? High school students looking for a band to play at parties? Event coordinators who need dancers?
- Industry description. What does the music/dance/theater industry look like right now, and how do you fit in?
- Product/service description. Explain what sort of art you're offering, and how much you'll charge for performances, teaching, or speaking about your art. How will you deliver your service?
- Marketing plan. You'll need to know how you're going to advertise.
- Competition. Who will you be competing with? What makes you stand out?

Research Project

Look around the Internet for examples of performing arts businesses. Do some Google searches or check your local yellow pages online or in a physical copy. You might find a singer who offers lessons, a band that performs at weddings, or a dancer that does freelance work. Explore their website and see what's on there. Write down all the things you can find that you think are important for a performing arts business website.

else. If you have a band, for example, you should talk about how you're all going to work together. Who will host practices? Who's going to look for work? What will happen if someone has to drop out? Figuring that stuff out now will help you out down the road.

An important part of a performing arts business is marketing and advertising. You could be an amazing performer, but other people have to know that too. Set up a website and get on social media sites like Facebook and Twitter. Post ads for your business around town or online. The more time you spend on marketing and advertising, the more visible you'll be to potential audiences.

NETWORKING

Finally, if you're trying to break into the performing arts, you'll need to network. That means you'll need to connect with lots and lots of people who can help you. You might meet with people who are already established artists. They can give you advice, and may even offer to mentor you or steer you toward jobs. People in the field of performing arts might let you know about performance gigs that aren't posted to the general

Text-Dependent Questions

1. What sorts of educational opportunities can you look for in the performing arts, as a young person right now?
2. Which performing artists need to go to college for their art?
3. Why is practicing so important?
4. Describe at least three parts to a business plan.
5. What is networking, and how will it help you?

public, or let you know when a group is looking for a new member. Always be open to new acquaintances, since you never know how you can help each other out.

Networking with other young performing artists is great too. You never know who will become successful, and if you happen to be friends with someone who find some success, he might be able to help you out as well. You can form new bands, new orchestras, new dance groups, and new theater companies with other young performing artists.

As you can see, the performing arts involves quite a lot—the actual performances, practicing, advertising, networking, and more. Dance, theater, music, and more may look very different from the origins of each performing art, but they still inspire and move people in ways that haven't changed much through the years. If you want to be involved in the performing arts as a hobby or even a career, stick with it, and you just might be successful.

Find Out More

Online

Arts Alive
www.artsalive.ca/en/dan/dance101/whydance.asp

Kids Work! History of the Theater
knowitall.org/kidswork/theater/history/index.html

Music
kids.usa.gov/teens-home/music/index.shtml

U.S. Bureau of Labor Statistics Occupational Outlook Handbook: Entertainment and Sports Occupations.
www.bls.gov/ooh/entertainment-and-sports/home.htm

wiseGeek: What Are the Different Types of Performing Arts?
www.wisegeek.com/what-are-the-different-types-of-performing-arts.htm

In Books

DK Publishing. *Dance.* New York: DK Publishing, 2012.

Ferguson. *Performing Arts (Discovering Careers for Your Future).* New York: Ferguson Publishing, 2005.

Mayfield, Katherine. *Acting A to Z: The Young Person's Guide to a Stage or Screen Career.* New York: Back Stage Books, 2010.

Nathan, Amy. *The Young Musician's Survival Guide*. New York: Oxford University Press, 2008.

Guerinot, Jim, Jared Levine, Robbie Robertson, and Sebastian Robertson. *Legends, Icons, and Rebels: Music that Changed the World*. Plattsburg, N.Y.: Tundra Books, 2013.

Series Glossary of Key Terms

Abstract: Made up of shapes that are symbolic. You might not be able to tell what a piece of abstract art is just by looking at it.

Classical: A certain kind of art traditional to the ancient Greek and Roman civilizations. In music, it refers to music in a European tradition that includes opera and symphony and that is generally considered more serious than other kinds of music.

Culture: All the arts, social meanings, thoughts, and behaviors that are common in a certain country or group.

Gallery: A room or a building that displays art.

Genre: A category of art, all with similar characteristics or styles.

Impressionism: A style of painting that focuses more on the artist's perception of movement and lighting than what something actually looks like.

Improvisation: Created without planning or preparation.

Medium (media): The materials or techniques used to create a work of art. Oil paints are a medium. So is digital photography.

Pitch: How high or low a musical note is; where it falls on a scale.

Portfolio: A collection of some of the art an artist has created, to show off her talents.

Realism: Art that tries to show something exactly as it appears in real life.

Renaissance: A period of rapid artistic and literary development during the 1500s–1700s, or the name of the artistic style from this period.

Studio: A place where an artist can work and create his art.

Style: A certain way of creating art specific to a person or time period.

Technique: A certain way of creating a piece of art.

Tempo: How fast a piece of music goes.

Venue: The location or facility where an event takes place.

Index

About the Author

Z.B. Hill is a an author and publicist living in Binghamton, New York. He has a special interest in education and how art can be used in the classroom.

Picture Credits

Dreamstime.com:
8: Telecast
18: Julia Fikse
30: Maxirf
34: Photographerlondon
36: Katkov
40: Edward Karaa
41: Tatiana Morozova
44: Thomas Lammeyer
46: Jesse Kunerth
47: Monkey Business Images
48: Pavel Losevsky
50: Barbara Reddoch

Fotolia.com:
6: Alexander Yakovlev

10: Andrey Armyagov
12: KABUGUI
13: nyul
32: Jean-Paul Bouninep2
38: Кирилл Рыжов
52: ova
54: Serg Nvns

16: Yorck Project
20: Margaret Herrick Library
24: U.S. Library of Congress
26: George Chernilevsky